URQUHART · CASTLE
Loch Ness

Chris Tabraham

Principal Inspector of Ancient Monument

Edited by Chris Tabraham

Designed by Studioarc

Main photography by Mike Brooks and David Henrie

of Historic Scotland's Photographic Unit

Illustrated by David Simon, Jan Tabraham

and Mike Moore

Published by HISTORIC SCOTLAND

Crown Copyright © Historic Scotland 2002

First published 2002

Printed in Scotland from sustainable material by

Scotprint, Haddington

HISTORIC SCOTLAND

ISBN 1 903570 30 1

Loch Ness, looking to the north-east

(Photograph © Colin Baxter)

A·GUIDED·TOUR

Urquhart Castle was a large and complex place. Residential and social considerations dictated its size and layout as much as defensive ones.

Urquhart Castle was a major place of strength. It endured much hostile action, and was constantly being repaired and rebuilt. But Urquhart was also a nobleman's residence, and successive owners took every opportunity to improve their accommodation.

The most significant improvement was the relocation of the 'heart' of the castle - the lord and lady's own quarters - from the high ground, the summit, in the southern half of

the site down to the more accessible, and less exposed, area in the northern half. This wholesale change seems to have been carried through during the fourteenth century.

Alas, much of the dressed stonework, used for features such as doors, windows and fireplaces, was later robbed for use elsewhere in the glen. As a result, there is little architectural detail, other than in the Grant Tower, to help date the various parts of the ruined complex.

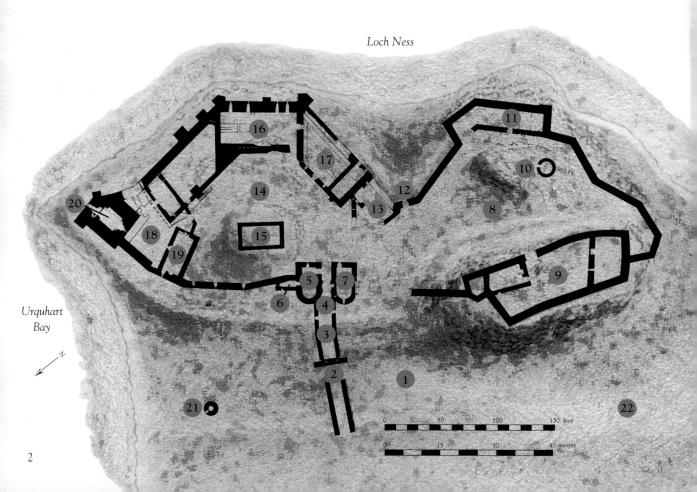

2

This tour takes the visitor around the castle ruins, pointing out the features of interest. It begins at the drawbridge and ditch on the landward side (in the foreground in the aerial view) and ends at the impressive Grant Tower, at the north end of the promontory (on the far left in the aerial view). From there one can get the most magnificent views over Loch Ness and the majestic scenery of the Great Glen.

Urquhart Castle from the north-west

Key to Castle Plan

1	Ditch	7	Kiln	13	Stable?	19	Kitchen
2	Drawbridge (site of)	8	Service Close	14	Outer Close	20	Grant Tower
3	Causeway	9	Summit	15	Chapel?	21	Kiln
4	Gatehouse	10	Dovecot	16	Great Hall cellars	22	Site of castle-toun
5	Guard room	11	Smithy?	17	Kitchens		
6	Prison	12	Water Gate	18	Inner Close		

The Ditch and Drawbridge

The castle stands on a rugged and irregular hourglass-shaped promontory jutting into the ice-cold waters of Loch Ness. The landward side of the promontory was defended by a rock-cut **ditch**, 30 m across at its widest point and 5 m deep on average. The ditch has clearly been widened and deepened during its long history.

A stone causeway crosses the ditch, and a modern fixed bridge now spans the gap where the **drawbridge** used to be. Exactly what that drawbridge looked like is unclear. That it was a heavy and robust structure operated from the castle side of the ditch is clear from the surviving features - the large vertical sockets for timber uprights, and the stone buttresses for counteracting the immense thrust of the timbers and lifting mechanism.

The **causeway** between the drawbridge and gatehouse was enclosed within stone walls. Now just mere footings, they were once fitted with arrow-slits and gates, or sallyports, through which the garrison could 'sally forth' to engage the enemy whilst the drawbridge remained raised and barred.

The ditch and drawbridge as they might have looked (from the model by Jim Masson in the Castle Visitor Centre)

The gatehouse from the outer close

The Gatehouse

Only the lower two storeys of the twin-towered **gatehouse** remain more-or-less intact. The upper levels, including the battlements, came crashing to the ground, possibly after the Jacobite Rising in 1689-90. Parts from those upper storeys lie on the grass in front of the gatehouse; they incorporate chimney flues and latrine chutes.

The gatehouse controlled entry into the castle and provided residential accommodation on the upper floors.

At ground level is the **entrance passage**, wide enough to allow carts to pass through. It was strongly defended. A portcullis protected the outer portal - the grooves for it can still be seen; it was raised and lowered from an upper floor. Further into the passage were two more barriers, either stout timber doors or open-barred iron grilles, called yetts in Scots; one opened outwards, the other inwards. The passage between the portcullis and these inner doors was covered over by a timber deck containing 'murder holes', through which the garrison could shoot down on the attacking force trying to break in.

*The **porter** kept the keys to the Castle*

The Guard Room

On the north side of the passage (on the left as you enter) a door leads to the **guard room** or porter's lodge. The porter was the medieval equivalent of today's security guard, controlling entry into the castle, checking visitors' credentials during the day and ensuring all was securely locked and barred at night. He also guarded any prisoners in the **prison cell** at the rear of his lodge. The long, narrow cell has a latrine at the far end.

A second gatehouse lodge, in the south tower and entered from the courtyard, was later converted into a **kiln-house**, where corn was dried, stored and ground into meal or flour.

The Constable's Lodging

The **first floor** of the gatehouse, now reached by the modern spiral stair in the porter's lodge, comprises a two-roomed **lodging**, a hall and chamber, with a latrine closet attached. This was most probably the lodging of the constable, or keeper of the castle, and from where he could control access into the castle. The hall, over the porter's lodge, was the equivalent of our living room, whilst the chamber, above the kiln-house, was a retiring room where he also slept, on a bed in the large wall cupboard. Both rooms had fireplaces and latrines. The odd space between the two rooms, directly over the entrance passage, originally gave access via a stair (a couple of treads remain in the wall) to the room high over the outer portal that housed the winding mechanism for the portcullis.

*The **constable** was the keeper of the Castle*

Boatmen *ferried goods to and from the castle via the water gate*

The Water Gate

At the narrow waist of the promontory, almost directly opposite the gatehouse, is the **water gate**. This gate gave access to the loch shore and was an important means of entry, and exit, in medieval times. In an age when roads were almost non-existent, most of the castle's provisions came by boat and were offloaded below the water gate. During the siege of the castle in 1689-90, the garrison was temporarily relieved by men and provisions successfully disembarking 'verry safe' at the water gate.

The Service Close

To the south (right) of the gatehouse is the highest part of the promontory. This summit area may have formed the focus of a well-defended Pictish stronghold in the first millennium AD. Quantities of vitrified stone* have been found on its slopes. The summit was probably also the heart of the first castle, built in the thirteenth century. But that heart clearly shifted later to the lower ground to the north of the gatehouse. Thereafter, the southern half was downgraded to a service close**. A cross-wall, now largely gone, running between the gatehouse and the water gate screened off the service close from the rest of the castle.

The footprint of a building to the north (left) of the water gate may have been a **stable**; although clearly an addition, it is in the most convenient place - just inside the service close near where the lord, lady and visiting guests would have dismounted on entering the outer close.

The stone walls on the **summit** are a confusing web of masonry devoid of any features that might help us to interpret them. The one recognisable structure is the circular **dovecot** on the terrace below the summit. Typical of sixteenth-century Scottish dovecots, it is almost certainly the 'dove-grove' referred to in the 1509 charter. Four nesting-boxes for the 'doos' (pigeons) survive. Dovecots were common features in medieval castles, providing a regular supply of pigeon meat and eggs for the lord's table, particularly through the long, harsh winter months.

Poulterers *tended to the 'doos' in the castle dovecot*

* **vitrified stone** - a glass-like material produced by intense heat and associated with late prehistoric forts.
** **close** - the Scots word for a courtyard.

The water gate (left centre) and gatehouse beyond

The only other significant surviving structure in the service close overlooks the loch. Its ground floor has previously been interpreted as a **smithy**, and it is possible that this was what it had become late in the castle's life. But the building clearly started out in the thirteenth century as one of high quality, perhaps a **great hall** or **guest range** to complement the lord's private accommodation on the summit. The ground-floor hearth could just as easily have served a kitchen (the scar of the wide chimney flue can be seen rising up through the masonry).

The upper floors were entered from the courtyard across what must have been a fine timber gallery, supported on large timbers held in the sockets still visible in the wall footings. The latrine closet high up in the surviving south-west corner (far right) confirms that this was no humble building.

The castle and Loch Ness from the summit

The outer close and Grant Tower from the service close

The Outer Close

By 1400 the 'heart' of the castle had moved to the northern half of the promontory (on the left from the gatehouse). After 1509, the Grants further developed the far, north end for their private lodging, the Grant Tower, thus forming two closes, an outer and an inner one.

The **outer close** is defined by the stone curtain wall skirting the outer edge of the rock. The section around the landward side survives almost to wallhead height, and has various arrow-slits through it.

The great hall cellars in the outer close from the top of the Grant Tower. The summit lies beyond

The Chapel

On top of the rocky knoll in the outer close are the foundations of a rectangular building. It may have been a **chapel**, although the orientation is more north-south than east-west, not what we would expect in a Christian building. The 'chapel' may originate from the time when the promontory was a Pictish fortress; St Columba baptised a Pictish nobleman and his family here around AD 580. It was normal for a large medieval castle to have its own place of worship, to save the castle residents from having to trek to the parish church, situated where Drumnadrochit village is today.

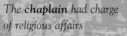

*The **chaplain** had charge of religious affairs*

The Great Hall

A medieval nobleman required much more in the way of accommodation than his own private lodging. Second only in importance to his own residence was the **great hall**, a spacious room used for various purposes, but chiefly as banqueting hall and courthouse (the lord was responsible for law and order in his barony). The great hall was situated along the east side of the outer close overlooking the loch. In addition to the large hall, there would have been a dais chamber, or retiring room, entered from the 'top', or lordly, end of the hall, The kitchens and storerooms were beyond the 'bottom' end and below.

***Carters** were a common sight in the outer close, loading and unloading goods into the castle's storage cellars*

A medieval nobleman's life was lived largely at first-floor level - the *piano nobile*, or noble floor - and the great hall at Urquhart was no exception. Sadly, little survives other than the sills of four great windows that lit the hall from the east, giving stunning views across the loch. The undercrofts, or **storage cellars**, are more complete. But as with the ruined buildings in the service close, they defy more precise interpretation. The **kitchens** seem to have been housed in the southern end, nearest the gatehouse and furthest from the lord's residence. The four small oblong windows lighting the cellars directly beneath the great hall are among the few surviving pieces of architectural detail, and their 'shouldered' internal lintels give us the clue that this block probably dates from the fourteenth century.

*The indispensible **alewife** tests the strength of her latest brew*

The Inner Close

Beyond the outer close lies the **inner close**, a small cobbled courtyard dominated by the lofty Grant Tower on the north (far) side. This close was the most important of the three courtyards. It was therefore walled off from the outer close and entry into it barred by a gate; both are now just low footings. A stone gutter still drains the close of rainwater.

Two other buildings were accessed off the close. Little can be said about the building on the east (right) side other than that its undercroft was probably a storeroom. The building on the west (left) side has a fireplace at either end, indicating that this was perhaps the 'kitchen' referred to in the 1509 charter. Until the later sixteenth century, most Scottish tower houses did not possess 'fitted kitchens', and the Grant Tower was no exception. The kitchen building was two storeys high, with additional living accommodation on the upper floor.

The inner close and Grant Tower

The Grant Tower

The most prominent feature of the entire castle is the tower house at the northern end of the promontory. It is now popularly known as the Grant Tower, after the family who built it. In 1509 Sir John Grant was held bound 'to repair or build at the castle a tower'.

The massively-thick basement walls possibly predate the Grants' arrival on the scene. It also seems likely that the parapets and turrets at the top are later alterations, carried out towards the close of the sixteenth century, or even into the seventeenth. The refinement may even have been the handiwork of James Moray, master-mason, who was carrying out major repairs at the castle as late as 1623. Despite the collapse of much of the tower's south wall, probably during a 'storme of wind' in February 1715, the building retains much of its sense of space and grandeur as a residence of nobility.

*The **cook** was master of his kitchen, presiding over the many kitchen hands and undercooks who served the household*

(right) The ruined Grant Tower is picked out by the winter sun

10

Access to the Grant Tower was extremely limited and security measures strong. A deep, stone-lined ditch along the two sides facing the inner close (the stretch along the south side was later filled in) increased the building's defence. The weakest point, the **entrance doorway**, must only have been reached by a removable bridge, whilst high above, at the wall-head, a projecting stone platform, carried on four stone corbels, enabled those within to 'cover' the entrance.

The Grant Tower is five storeys high, and the entrance door leads into the second of these, the **hall**. This was the least restricted of the rooms in the tower, an outer reception room that may also have been put to limited use for dining. It was lit by good-sized windows and heated by a large fireplace in the south wall. A narrow spiral stair leads down to a dimly-lit stone-vaulted **storeroom** in the basement and a well-defended **postern**, or back entry. A second spiral stair leads to the upper floors.

We do not know quite how the Grants used these **upper floors**, but we can speculate. The fine room directly over the hall was most likely their **outer chamber**, an altogether more private space, where the lord and lady could relax and entertain close friends. They would have dined here when not entertaining in the great hall. Above that again was their **inner chamber**, also a reception room but one reserved for their most intimate companions. It would also have contained their elaborate four-poster bed.

The topmost storey had a **garret** in the main tower, perhaps used by the servants, and pretty, square-gabled **turrets** at the corners, each containing a little chamber, complete with fireplace and window. Where once lords and ladies admired the view, now countless visitors can do likewise.

*The lord and lady (above) were attended by many servants. The **lady-in-waiting** (right) was her ladyship's constant companion, while the **wardrober** (below) looked after the noble couple's expensive garments*

*The lord's **'freindis'** spent many happy hours in their lord's hall*

Most of the tower windows have pistol-holes below their sills

A cut-open reconstruction of the Grant Tower showing how the various floors may have been used (illustration by David Simon)

THE·STORY·OF
URQUHART·CASTLE

'The famous castel of Urquhart:
of quhilk the rewinous wallis remains
yet in great admiration of pepill.'

(Hector Boece, Principal of Aberdeen University,
in his *History of Scotland*, 1527)

The rocky promontory jutting into the chilly depths of Loch Ness on which the noble ruined castle of Urquhart stands has played host to some famous names.

St Columba visited with peaceful intent around AD 580. Not so Edward I of England, 'Hammer of the Scots', who seized the castle in 1296. The MacDonald Lords of the Isles stormed through the glen time and again in the later Middle Ages, ruling with a rod of iron from the castle.

In the twilight of its days as a lordly seat of the chiefs of Grant, Urquhart continued to prove its worth as a stronghold. Last garrisoned in 1689, it was said that the towering gatehouse was blown up so that the castle could never again be a military stronghold. Over 1500 years of stirring history were buried beneath the rubble.

A·FORTRESS·OF·THE·PICTS

Around AD 580, St Columba visited Urquhart. The noble Pict whom he baptised there was one in a long line of lords who for centuries had ruled over the glen from the promontory jutting into Loch Ness.

Urquhart* steps onto the pages of history around AD 580. St. Columba, founder of the monastery on Iona in Argyllshire, was making a long and tiring journey to the court of Bridei, king of the Picts**, at Inverness. His mission was to bring Christianity to them. To reach his destination, the holy man had to travel up Loch Ness. As he was passing Glen Urquhart, he was called to the residence of an elderly Pictish nobleman who was close to death.

St Columba baptises the Pict, Emchath, on his death-bed; an artist's impression (David Simon)

'When the holy man, Columba, was beside the lake of the River Ness, in the province of the Picts, he went to the estate which is called Airdchartdan [Urquhart]. And a certain old man whom he found there, Emchath, hearing and believing the word of God preached by the saint, was baptised.'

(Abbot Adomnan's *Life of Columba*, written around AD 690)

Columba baptised not only Emchath but his whole household. The holy man evidently got there just in time for Emchath thereafter 'gladly and confidently departed to the Lord'.

A Pictish burial at Garbeg; an artist's impression (Mike Moore)

* **Urquhart** - anciently Airdchartdan (7th century), from Gaelic *air* 'by' and Old Welsh *cardden*, 'a thicket or wood' = 'by the wood'.

** **Picts** - Scotland's oldest people. The Romans called them *Picti*, 'Painted Ones'. By St. Columba's time they were a confederation of tribes inhabiting most of Scotland north of the Firth of Forth. Around 843 they were united with the Scots under Kenneth mac Alpin.

There is no certainty that Emchath's residence was on the rocky promontory. However, the discovery there of a fragment of Pictish brooch has led to speculation that his residence was where the ruined castle now stands. The discovery of pieces of vitrified rock on the slopes of the summit confirms that the promontory was a well-fortified place around Columba's time. It was an ideal site for a fort - surrounded on three sides by the deep waters of the loch, easily defended from the landward side, and commanding extensive views.

We know there were Picts living in fertile Glen Urquhart. A number of place-names are Pictish in origin (eg Pitkerrald - *pit* meant 'farm' or 'share', hence 'Cyril's farm'; Duldreggan - *dul* meant 'meadow', hence 'meadow of the dragon?'). Although little now survives of the homes of the Picts, one of their burial grounds has been found at Garbeg, just 2 miles (3 km) from the castle, on ground overlooking the village of Drumnadrochit.

The fragment of Pictish brooch (late 8th - early 9th century) found at the castle in the nineteenth century (Courtesy of Inverness Museum and Art Gallery)

Columba and the Water-Beast

St•Columba

Today, people visit Urquhart Castle not only to view the ruins of a once-mighty medieval castle but to try to catch a glimpse of the famous 'Loch Ness Monster'. Tales of mythical water-beasts have long been associated with Highland lochs. But the sighting of a monster in or around Loch Ness was first recorded in Columba's time. His biographer, Adomnan, describes the unforgettable moment in the life of the holy man:

'When Columba reached the river bank, he saw a poor fellow being buried; and the buriers said that, while swimming, the man had been seized and most savagely bitten by a water beast [aquatilis bestia].

Notwithstanding, the holy man ordered Lugne, one of his companions, to swim across to the other side and bring back a boat. Lugne obeyed without delay, but the monster . . . suddenly swam to the surface and with gaping mouth and great roaring rushed towards the man in midstream.

While all there were struck down with extreme terror, the blessed man raised his holy hand and commanded the savage beast: "Do not touch the man; turn back speedily." The beast, as if pulled back with ropes, fled terrified in swift retreat.

The brothers with great amazement glorified God, and also the pagan barbarians [Picts] who were there at the time.'

THE·FIRST·CASTLE

In the early thirteenth century, following the quelling of an uprising in Moray, King Alexander II granted the lordship of Urquhart to the powerful Durward family. They built the first castle.

In 1228, the 'men of Moray' - a huge province of Scotland reaching from the North Sea to the Atlantic coast - rose up against their king. King Alexander II ruthlessly crushed the rebellion, and by Christmas 1230 he was in Elgin celebrating his victory.

The king straightaway began bringing in men he could trust to help him secure the rebellious province. He granted the large and sprawling lordship of Urquhart* to Sir Thomas 'le Durward'. Thomas died soon after and his new prize passed to his son, Alan, the king's son-in-law. It was probably Sir Alan who built the first castle.

Thomas and Alan were descended from Normans who had come to Scotland in the twelfth century. They held the prestigious post of usher, or door-ward (door-keeper), at the royal court - hence their surname. Alan Durward was already Earl of Atholl, claimant to the earldom of Mar, and holder of extensive estates in Angus, the Mearns and Mar (a great slice of eastern Scotland), as well as the stately castle and broad acres of Bolsover in the English Midlands. For many years thereafter he was the real power behind the throne.

If a castle existed at Urquhart before the Durwards came there, there is no mention of it in the records and no evidence of it on the ground. But for Sir Alan to secure his lordship against a hostile population, he certainly needed an impregnable fortress. Some parts of the present ruin were certainly built for him, including the great ditch on the landward side and stretches of the perimeter wall.

(above) A charter bearing the seal of Alan Durward
(right) A bone gaming piece showing a horseman found at Urquhart and possibly dating from the Durward occupation

---

* **Urquhart** - the surname 'Urquhart' derives not from the Urquhart beside Loch Ness but from another place called Urquhart in Cromarty, north of Inverness; the Urquharts became hereditary sheriffs of Cromarty from the early fourteenth century. There was, however, an association between the surname and the castle that coincidentally bears their name - Gylleroch de Urchard appears as witness to the 1233 agreement between Sir Alan le Durward and the Church of Urquhart.

The Peel Ring of Lumphanan, in Aberdeenshire, fringed by the trees, was also a Durward stronghold, probably a hunting lodge. King Macbeth, one of Moray's greatest sons, was killed nearby in 1057. The peel is in Historic Scotland's care

The Durwards took their family name from the prestigious post of **door-ward**, or door-keeper, at the royal court

A key found at Urquhart Castle

'That noble man [Sir Alan], for the sake of peace, has given to the church of Urquhart half the lands claimed, in pure, free, and perpetual charity. But he and his heirs will possess the other half in perpetual feufarm.'

(the Register of the Diocese of Moray, March 1233)

Sir Alan Durward

THE·CASTLE·AS·RESIDENCE

Urquhart Castle was not just a stronghold. It was also the occasional residence of a nobleman, his lady and their large retinue. It served also as hotel, estate office, barracks, law court and prison.

Urquhart Castle never served as the main residence of its noble lord. The chief seat of the Durwards was at Coull, in Aberdeenshire, and the Grants, who held Urquhart in the twilight of its days, resided mainly at Freuchie (now Castle Grant), beside Grantown-on-Spey. For most of the period in between, Urquhart was a royal castle, though only one king of Scots ever slept there - David II in 1342. For much of that time the castle was looked after by a keeper, or trusted lieutenant, generally a local knight, who could be relied on to do his king's bidding. When the MacDonald Lords of the Isles held the castle, they too rarely stayed there, relying like the king on faithful henchmen to maintain the stronghold in readiness for their coming.

A clump of corroded arrowheads found at Urquhart Castle. The pouch which held them has long since rotted. (inset) One of the many arrowheads found at Urquhart

Mighty noblemen like the Durwards, MacDonalds and Grants were constantly on the move, attending their king and sittings of parliament, visiting their peers (social equals), and fighting wars. They also had to visit their various estates frequently, to dispense justice and consume their rents, most of which were paid in kind (corn and animals) not cash. Urquhart though had a special attraction for any owner, for it gave him unlimited access to one of the best hunting reserves in Scotland, the royal forest of Cluanie, which the lord of Urquhart administered on his sovereign's behalf.

An ornate ring brooch (above) and a rowel spur (right) both found at Urquhart Castle. They date from the fourteenth or fifteenth century

THE · LORD'S · HOUSEHOLD

Freindis (social equals)　　**Kin (blood relations)**　　## Lord

🔑 Constable　　☾ Marshal　　✝ Chaplain

Gunners　Doorwards　　Blacksmiths　Carters　　Clerk of the Writing Office　Clerk of the Chapel

Men-at-Arms　　Farriers　Messengers　Muleteers　　Assistant Clerks　Sacristan

Armourers　Porters　　Boatmen　　Stable Lads　　Choir Boys

Serv

22

Lady

Tenentis (tenants)

🏺 **Steward** ⚱️

Cook Bard Piper Doctor Gentlemen Ladies-in-
                                Servants   Waiting

Musicians Stonemasons Carpenters Wardrobers Tailor Laundress

Undercooks Larderers Bakers Alewife Poulterers Gardeners

dis

23

'. . . kin, freindis, tenentis, servandis and dependaris . . .'

(the marriage contract between Sir John Grant of Freuchie, future owner of Urquhart Castle,
and Lady Margaret Ogilvie of Deskford, dated 1483)

Wherever the lord went he was accompanied by his 'household' - his officials and servants.

Urquhart was crowded, warm, noisy - and smelly - only when its master was in residence. At all other times it would have had a sepulchral feel about it. It would also have been largely empty of possessions, for not only did the household follow their lord around, so too did most of his furniture and furnishings. Everything more or less had to be capable of being stowed in the baggage-train and carried from place to place - pots and pans, linen and wall-hangings, as well as bulky items of furniture such as the lord's 'board' (dining table), chair of state, and great four-poster bed.

*The **marshal** (above) and the **farriers** helped keep the lord on the move*

We have no details for any household of the noble families that held Urquhart. However, evidence from elsewhere in Scotland suggests a household of well over 100 people. Picture the hectic scene during David II's visit in the summer of 1342. Not only was the sovereign and his travelling household in residence, but also two bishops (Moray and Ross) and three lords (Sir Robert de Lauder, Sir John de Kerdale and Sir William de Moubray), each with his own household - upwards of 300 men and horses.

24

The size and complex layout of the ruined castle still convey something of its former grandeur. It is one of the largest castles in Scotland, though to an extent that is determined by the physical nature of the site. Three closes, or courtyards, define the hierarchy of lordship:

- an **outer close**, dominated by its great hall where all those seeking access to the lord could go;
- an **inner close**, housing the lord and lady's private lodgings which only those and such as those were permitted to enter;
- a **service close**, crowded with stables, storerooms and other outbuildings where most of the lower orders in the household worked.

*The **steward** was master of the household and oversaw the day-to-day running of the castle*

But that was not the physical limit of the castle. Beyond the great ditch, on the landward side, was the formal approach to the drawbridge. By the seventeenth century this seems to have been along a very presentable avenue of trees surrounded by gardens and orchards. Also beyond the castle ditch was the **castle-toun**, or settlement. This was an extension of the service close within the precinct walls, where less salubrious activities such as smithing were carried on and where pigs and hens rootled and scratched about among the middens (rubbish heaps). The large **corn-kiln** in the far north end of the ditch, built late on in the castle's history, is evidence of this castle-toun, and recent archaeological excavations have unearthed traces of other light-industry and the foundations of flimsy timber buildings.

This new archaeological evidence is helping to 'flesh out' the light shed by documents. The 1509 charter lists buildings such as the hall, chamber, kitchen, pantry, bakehouse, brewhouse, barn, oxhouse, kiln, dovecot and orchard. Sprinkled about elsewhere are references to members of the Grant household, including an armourer, *An Gobhan More* (literally 'the big smith'), a chaplain, Alexander Farquharson, who was at the first chief of Grant's deathbed in 1528, and Donald the piper in 1624.

*The **piper** (above) was always in attendance on his lord. **Blacksmiths** (below) were central figures 'behind the scenes'*

THE·ESTATE·OF·URQUHART

Urquhart Castle was the centre of a vast estate reaching from Loch Ness far into the mountains to the west. The lord of Urquhart controlled everything that moved or grew in the lordship.

There are no details of the extent of the estate, or lordship, granted to the Durwards in the 1230s. However, thanks to the survival of royal charters granted to Sir James Grant and his two sons in 1509, we have a remarkably accurate picture both of the extent of the ancient lordship and of the settlements within it at that time.

The estate was vast, covering an area roughly the size of the Isle of Man. It enveloped both Glen Urquhart and Glen Moriston to its south, and extended from the fertile corn-lands beside Loch Ness inland over good pasture as far as the rich hunting-grounds of the Cluanie Forest high in the mountains to the west. The high proportion of deer bones, almost 10%, found in archaeological excavations at the castle, demonstrates how valued hunting was in medieval times.

The lord's own 'desmesne', or domain (from the French *de main* 'of the hand', from which we get the place-name Mains, 'home farm'), which he farmed at his own hand, was located on the higher ground overlooking the castle to the west. It comprised four fermtouns, or farming townships - Borlum (a corruption of 'boardland', board being the lord's table; hence 'board and lodgings'), Strone, Clunebeg and Boglashin.

Much of the human settlement elsewhere in the estate was clustered in lower Glen Urquhart, on the fertile soil beside where the gushing waters of the River Enrick flow into Urquhart Bay. There, a number of fermtouns were all sited within walking distance of the parish church, St Ninian's, a fragment of which survives in Drumnadrochit. The fermtoun names, derived from either Gaelic or Pictish, belie their ancient roots. For example, Corrimony (Gaelic - *Còire Mhònaidh*, 'Monie's cauldron) most likely refers to the Bronze-Age cairn there. Glen Moriston was noticeably less intensively settled and farmed. Dr Johnson and Boswell visited the inn at Aonach, high up in the mountains, in 1773.

'. . . and to till or reclaim wild land in meadows and pastures, make enclosures, improve the public highway and supervise and care for the common benefits, such as stone and wooden bridges, fold-gates and stiles.'

(excerpt from James IV's charter to the first chief of Clan Grant of the estate of Urquhart, sealed at Stirling Castle, 8 December 1509)

(right) The promontory of Urquhart and Loch Ness from the north side of Urquhart Bay

The 1509 charters also mention the shieling grounds, or summer grazings, dotted about the royal forest of Cluanie in the mountains to the west. This reminds us that each May the younger members of the family (the wife and children mostly) went with their cattle and goats into the upland pastures for the summer, leaving the husband and grandparents back home to tend the crops and 'house-sit'. Only after the harvest was safely gathered in did they return.

The lord of Urquhart held all this of his sovereign, in return for ensuring that good order prevailed, and that the estate contributed to the nation's economic well-being.

There was another royal expectation, and that was that the estate would contribute its share of military muscle whenever the king demanded it. What Sir Alan Durward was expected to bring to the 'host', or common army of Scotland, is not known, but in 1509 Sir James Grant was held bound to provide one lance and three horsemen for every parcel of land valued at £10 - a total of five lance and fifteen horsemen. Whether such a force was sent south four years later to join James IV's ill-fated expedition into northern England that resulted in disaster on Flodden Field is not known. However, listed among the fallen on that dreich September day was Master John Grant, the chief's son.

GLEN URQUHART

1 **Borlum** - from 'boardland'
2 **Strone** - *Sron*, 'nose or point'
3 **Clunebeg** - *A' Chluain Bheag*, 'little green meadowy pasture'
4 **Boglashin** - *Both Ghlas-bheinn*, 'hut of the grey rock'
5 **Tychat** - *Tigh a' Chait*, 'house of the cat'
6 **Kerrowgair** - *An Ceathramh Geàrr*, 'short quarter davach'
7 **Drumbuie** - *An Druim Buidhe*, 'yellow ridge'
8 **Balmacaan** - *Baile Mac Cathain*, 'Mac Cathan's homestead'
9 **Clunemore** - *A' Chluain Mhor*, 'large green meadowy pasture'
10 **Divach** - *Dhibheach?*, 'house of the (cattle) beasts'?
11 **Pitkerrald** - *Pit ?*, 'St Cyril's township'?
12 **Gartally** - *Car Dalaidh*, 'Daly's circle'
13 **Polmaily** - *Polla Mhàilidh*, 'St Màlie's pool'
14 **Delshangie** - *Dul ?*, 'narrow meadow'?
15 **Achtemarak** - *Ach' an t-Seamarag*, 'field of the shamrock'
16 **Lochletter** - *Lòch-leitir*, 'dark, wet hillside'
17 **The Four Meiklies** (*Miachdlaidh?*) including:
    Shewglie - *Seagalaidh*, 'place of rye';
    Craskaig - *Crasg*, 'little pass'
18 **Corrimony** - *Coire Mhònaidh*, 'Monie's cauldron'
19 **Bunloit** - *Bun Leothaid*, 'lower part of the broad hillside'

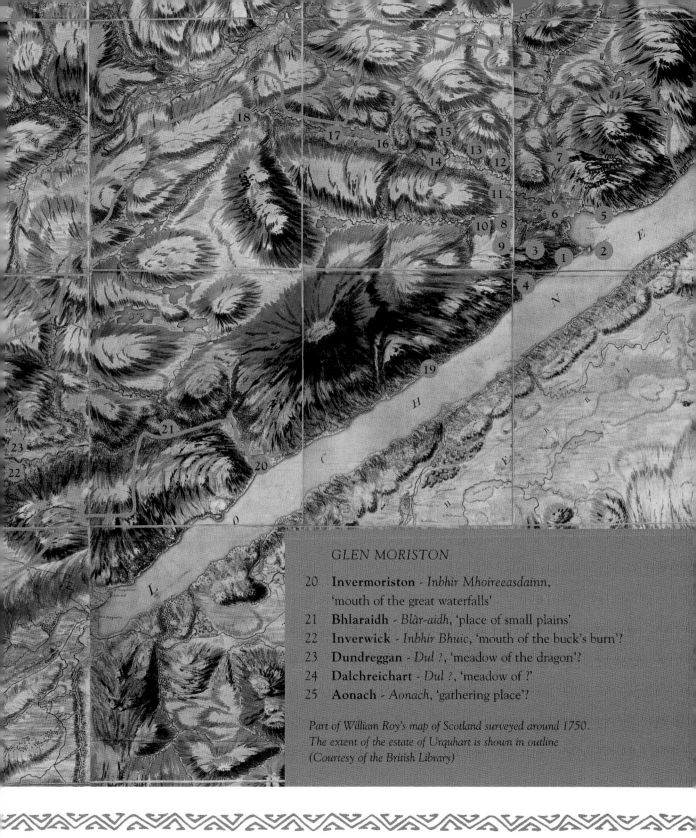

GLEN MORISTON

20 **Invermoriston** - *Inbhir Mhoireeasdainn*,
'mouth of the great waterfalls'
21 **Bhlaraidh** - *Blàr-aidh*, 'place of small plains'
22 **Inverwick** - *Inbhir Bhuic*, 'mouth of the buck's burn'?
23 **Dundreggan** - *Dul ?*, 'meadow of the dragon'?
24 **Dalchreichart** - *Dul ?*, 'meadow of ?'
25 **Aonach** - *Aonach*, 'gathering place'?

*Part of William Roy's map of Scotland surveyed around 1750.
The extent of the estate of Urquhart is shown in outline
(Courtesy of the British Library)*

URQUHART·AND·THE WARS·OF·INDEPENDENCE

For much of the time Urquhart would have been a peaceful place. But there were many times when that peace was shattered, beginning in 1296 and the Wars of Independence.

Alan Durward died without male heir in 1275. The king granted his castle and estate at Urquhart to another powerful 'incomer', John Comyn, lord of Badenoch and Lochaber. It proved a brief association for Scotland was soon embroiled in the bloody Wars of Independence* with England.

Edward I penny found at the castle

In March 1296, Edward I of England, 'Hammer of the Scots', invaded Scotland. By July he had reached Elgin. Scotland lay at his mercy, its army routed and its great castles captured. Urquhart was among them. Seizing castles was one thing; holding on to them proved more difficult. In the general rising of 1297, Sir Andrew de Moray, a powerful local nobleman, spearheaded a night attack on Urquhart, but was beaten off.

Undaunted, Moray marched south, and with William Wallace defeated the English at the Battle of Stirling Bridge. The English garrison holed up in Urquhart must have surrendered shortly after, for by the following year Urquhart was back in Scottish hands.

Back came the English. In 1303, Edward of England returned to Moray and retook Urquhart Castle despite Sir Alexander de Forbes's stout defence. Such was the confused state of loyalties that Edward was able to install Sir Alexander Comyn of Badenoch as his new constable. This time the English were

Sir Andrew de Moray

set for a longer stay, and in July 1306 we read of the garrison being supplied with wheat and wine. By then, though, Robert the Bruce had emerged from the shadows and been crowned King of Scots. In 1308, he swept through the northern part of his realm, annihilated his avowed enemy, the Comyns, and took control of their castles and lands, including Urquhart. Thereafter, little is heard of Urquhart for the rest of the Wars of Independence.

Edward I of England's army beseige Urquhart Castle 1296; an artist's impression (David Simon)

* **Wars of Independence** - a long struggle by the Scots to fight off attempts by three English kings to conquer Scotland. Beginning in 1296 with Edward I of England's invasion, it only effectively ended in 1357 with David II's return from captivity in the Tower of London.

A·ROYAL·CASTLE

The Wars of Independence resulted in Urquhart becoming a royal castle, held for the Crown by a succession of royal constables. Royalty rarely visited.

The downfall of the Comyns, the pro-English holders of Urquhart, early on in the Wars of Independence resulted in the Crown annexing the lordship of Urquhart. The castle then effectively became a royal castle.

There is one brief record of its role in the defence of Scotland during the dark days following Robert the Bruce's death in 1329. The defeat of the Scottish host in 1332 at Dupplin, near Perth, once more called into question the independence of Scotland. Mighty Urquhart Castle, alone of all the Highland castles, held out against the aggressor.

'The English resumed possession of the whole kingdom, excepting only five castles, that is Dumbarton, Loch Leven, Kildrummy, Loch Doon and Urquhart, whose keeper was Sir Robert de Lauder who was called "the Good".'

(from Abbot Bower's *Scotichronicon*, c.1440)

It proved to be the last occasion Urquhart was threatened by the English.

A succession of constables, or keepers, thereafter maintained the place in readiness for their king's coming. A great deal of money was spent by the exchequer keeping the place in good repair. However, the only 'royal' known to have visited was David II, Robert the Bruce's son, who bided there during the summer of 1342. Presumably the attraction was the chance to indulge in a spot of hunting in his royal forest of Cluanie.

David II, son of Robert the Bruce (left) greets his adversary Edward III of England. King David resided at Urquhart in the summer of 1342 (Courtesy of the British Library)

Men-at-arms *were skilled with the bow - long bow and crossbow - and the Lochaber Axe*

THE·URQUHART·EWER

'Remember the day we found the teapot?'
John McDonald of Glen Urquhart, Ministry of Works workman, 1921

This 'teapot' was found by workmen clearing the castle ruins in 1921. It is in fact a very fine example of a ewer, or water jug, probably made in the Netherlands in the fifteenth century. The bronze ewer once had a hinged lid, now lost.

Such an object took pride of place in the lord's hall. It would have been used by the lord and his guests for ritually cleansing their hands before sitting down to their meal. The Urquhart Ewer now takes pride of place in the Castle Visitor Centre.

(The ewer and other objects illustrated in this guide and on display in the Visitor Centre are on loan to Historic Scotland from the National Museums of Scotland)

URQUHART · AND · THE LORDS · OF · THE · ISLES

In 1395 Donald MacDonald, Lord of the Isles, seized the castle. Over the next 150 years the MacDonalds and their henchmen made life a misery for the people of Urquhart.

After the drama of Dupplin in 1332, Glen Urquhart and its castle returned to a state of calm. When the noise of war returned to the glen, it came not from the south and the kings of England but from the west and the Lords of the Isles.

The MacDonald Lords of the Isles exercised a powerful influence over a great swathe of the western seaboard of Scotland. As the fourteenth century drew to a close, they sought to extend it even further, by casting their covetous eyes over the earldom of Ross, to the north and east of their ancestral lands. Glen Urquhart was in the way. Time and again they swept through the glen, burning crops and homes, seizing cattle and anything else of value, and generally wreaking havoc. The castle passed back and forth between the Crown and the Lords of the Isles like a bone between two dogs.

The Lords of the Isles first appeared in the glen in 1395 when Donald MacDonald seized the lands of Urquhart and installed his henchman, Charles MacLean of Lochbuie, as keeper of its castle. The Crown made a feeble attempt to retake it but failed. MacLean was still holding sway when MacDonald himself marched by in 1411, on his ill-fated invasion of north-east Scotland.

Donald, Lord of the Isles

Oh, came ye frae the Hielans, man?
And came ye a' the wye?
Saw ye MacDonal and his men
Come marching frae the Skye?

(an old ballad recalling the Lord of the Isles' great raid in 1411 that culminated in the bloody Battle of Harlaw)

The Battle of Harlaw, near Inverurie in Aberdeenshire, was neither a victory nor a defeat. But the bloodshed spilled that day beside the River Don effectively stopped the MacDonald war-machine in its tracks. The Crown regained the initiative and drove them back over the mountains to the west. Urquhart returned into royal hands. It brought only temporary reprieve to the beleaguered inhabitants of the glen.

James I's murder in 1437 saw Donald MacDonald's successor, Alexander, wrest the estate back. He failed, however, to retake the castle. Exchequer accounts from the time show major expenditure on repair and new building at Urquhart to enable the royal garrison to cling on. An uneasy stand-off between the two warring parties ensued, broken in 1452 when Alexander's successor, John, then a high-spirited lad of 18, succeeded in seizing the castle. A compromise was reached whereby the lordship of Urquhart with its castle was granted by the Crown to John MacDonald for his lifetime only. Peace of a sort returned to the glen.

Lord John continued to further his ambition clandestinely. In 1462, he signed a pact with Edward IV of England whereby the Lord of the Isles would receive most of northern Scotland in return for supporting the English king. When news of the pact reached the ears of the Scottish king, James III, the latter was compelled to act. In 1476, John was stripped of his earldom of Ross, and the strategic castle of Urquhart was entrusted to George Gordon, second Earl of Huntly, then the most powerful figure in north-east Scotland.

If the inhabitants of Urquhart were expecting some respite following the years of unrest, they were to be disappointed. Continuing arguments over who held what from whom led to further devastation, so that by 1479 no rents at all were forthcoming from the lordship of Urquhart. In desperation, Huntly looked to one of his loyal supporters to take a grasp of the situation. When Sir Duncan Grant, Lord of Freuchie (now Castle Grant, beside Grantown-on-Spey), arrived in the glen in 1479, an association began that was to last for 500 years.

The gravestone in Kinkell Church, Inverurie, of Gilbert de Greenlaw, a lowlander killed at Harlaw in 1411 fighting the Lords of the Isles

URQUHART·AND·THE CHIEFS·OF·GRANTS

In 1509, the chief of Clan Grant was formally gifted Urquhart by a grateful king. Under the Grants, the castle became an active noble residence once more.

Sir Duncan Grant of Freuchie was an ageing warrior by the time he took on the lease of Urquhart, and he left it to his grandson, John, 'the Red Bard' (*Am Bard Ruadh*), to try to bring order to the troubled glen. By degrees he did so, for rents were soon flowing into the Crown coffers. His grateful sovereign, James IV, acknowledged the Bard's achievement, firstly in 1502 by offering him a five-year lease of Urquhart to be held directly of the Crown, and then, in 1509, by gifting the ancient lordship to the family in perpetuity. After 200 years in Crown hands, Urquhart was once again a baronial castle and seat of lordship.

'Know ye that for the increase of our rental . . . we have given, granted, and in feu-farme demitted, and, by this our present charter confirmed to our loving John Grant of Freuchie and his heirs male all and sundry the lands underwritten'

(James IV's charter to the first chief of Clan Grant of the lordship and castle of Urquhart, sealed at Stirling Castle, 8 December 1509)

Sir John Grant of Freuchie

The bestowal of this honour resulted in the vast lordship being divided into three. Sir John himself took the most lucrative portion, fertile Glen Urquhart, whilst two sons, Iain Og, 'young John', and Iain Mor, 'big John', received Corrimony, at the head of Glen Urquhart, and Glen Moriston respectively. The terms of the gifts left the three in no doubt as to what they were expected to achieve. The chief of Grant and his heirs 'are taken bound to repair or build at the castle a tower, with an outwork or rampart of stone and lime, for protecting the lands of the people from the inroads of thieves and malefactors.'

The chances of them realising their king's wishes immediately were slight for, despite the complete forfeiture of John, Lord of the Isles, in 1493 and his death five years later, the 'thieves and malefactors' from the west persisted.

James Grant (1616-1663), seventh Laird of Grant, and Mary Stewart, his wife, painted by David Scougall in 1658 (Courtesy of the National Museums of Scotland)

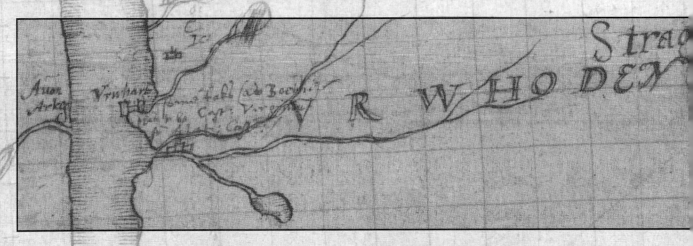

The earliest known illustration of Urquhart Castle, drawn by Timothy Pont - around 1580 (Courtesy of the National Library of Scotland)

The catalyst for renewed conflict was James IV's death at Flodden, in Northumberland, in 1513. The new 'Lord of the Isles', Donald MacDonald of Lochalsh, poured his clansmen once more into the glen, looting and killing, and capturing the castle. They stayed three years, stripping the inhabitants of all that they owned. When they eventually left, they took with them 300 cattle, 1000 sheep, countless sacks of barley and oats, and from the castle itself pots, pans, kettles, napery [linen], beds, sheets, blankets, coverings, fish, flesh, bread, ale, cheese, butter, salt hides and much else besides. Little wonder that when Hector Boece described the castle in 1528, he wrote of the castle's 'rewinous wallis'.

The 1545 'Great Raid' showing MacDonald's men carrying their booty to their boats via the castle's water gate; an artist's impression (David Simon)

THE·GREAT·RAID·OF·1545

Worse followed in 1545. This time a bloody encounter at Blar-na-Leine, beside Loch Lochy, was the immediate cause. The day-long battle between Lord Lovat's Frasers and the men from the west, in which the Grants and the men from Urquhart joined with the Frasers, saw both sides cut each other to pieces. In retaliation, the MacDonalds of Glengarry with the Camerons of Lochiel stormed again into the glen. A list of the plunder makes for sorry reading and shows why their attack became known as 'the Great Raid' - 2000 cattle, 383 horses, 3000 sheep, 2000 goats, 122 swine, 64 geese - and from the castle itself, 12 feather beds, with bolsters, blankets and sheets; brewing vats, roasting spits and yet more pots and pans; a chest containing £300; 20 guns, powder and stands of armour; yetts (iron gates); tables and other items of furniture; and three great boats.

The 'Great Raid' proved to be the last the inhabitants saw of the men from the west. Gradually the tenor of pastoral life was resumed in the glen, and the Grants began to repair the battered castle. They took the opportunity to build anew, as the lofty Grant Tower shows.

Urquhart Castle from the shore of Urquhart Bay

DECLINE·AND·FALL

As Urquhart declined as a residence, time took its toll on the ancient fabric. When the last soldiers marched out in 1692, they blew the place up.

By the seventeenth century the days of the castle as a noble residence were fast drawing to a close. Landowners throughout Scotland were abandoning their medieval castles and building more comfortable residences. The rocky promontory that had served their predecessors well no longer held any attraction for the chiefs of Grant.

The end came around Christmas 1644. Lady Mary Grant was residing in the castle when in stormed a band of Covenanters*, angry at Lady Mary's continuing loyalty to her sovereign, the beleaguered Charles I. They robbed her, rifled the castle of its contents and drove her ladyship out of her estate. She bemoaned: 'there is not left with me one serviette to eat my meat on'.

An inventory of the castle's contents, taken in 1647, confirms the castle's sorry state. The only items in the Grant Tower were - a bed, small table and bench in 'the chamber above the hall', a bed and table in 'the vault chamber', a large dining table, bench, table and chair in 'the hall', and in 'the cellar an old chest'. As for the rest of the once-mighty castle, it was 'without any kind of wares, planting, goods, or gear whatsoever . . . except only bare walls'.

Thereafter, the castle's decline was swift. Following Oliver Cromwell's invasion of Scotland in 1650, the English built new forts, called citadels, at either end of the Great Glen - Inverlochy (now Fort William) and Inverness. But they chose not to garrison Urquhart, content to patrol Loch Ness from a vessel, what one observer called 'a statly friggot'.

The castle was garrisoned for the final time 40 years later, during the troubles that followed James VII of Scotland's flight into exile in 1689. The chief of Grant, throwing in his lot with William and Mary, the new sovereigns, garrisoned Urquhart with three companies of Grant Highlanders, about 200 men in all.

Jacobite Soldier

* **Covenanters** - Scotland's Presbyterians during the religious turmoil of the seventeenth century. The name derived from the National Covenant of 1638, signed by over 300,000 Scots.

The floodlit castle, and (inset) a photograph of the gatehouse in 1957 showing the collapsed towers, brought down by an explosion in 1690. The fallen masonry has since been moved to one side, to improve access for visitors

Though they were poorly armed, 'having neither swords nor bayonets, and only a few carbines', they did have 'a fortnight's or three weeks' provisions'. They were soon besieged by a Jacobite** force more than twice their number. The garrison managed to hold out until the Jacobites' final defeat on the Haughs of Cromdale, above Grantown-on-Spey, in 1690.

When the soldiers finally marched out of the castle, they reportedly blew up some of the buildings to stop the enemy from holding it again. The results of their action are still visible in the great chunks of masonry lying beside the gatehouse. The damage was never repaired.

'I am certainly inform'd that 500 of the rebells were come to Urquett; they threatned the castle, but I looke upon it to be in little dainger, they [the garrison] haveing a fortnight's or three weeks's provisions.'

(despatch sent from Sir James Leslie to Lord Melville, commander of William II's Scottish army, on 6 December 1689, at the height of the first Jacobite Rising)

** **Jacobites** - supporters of the exiled Catholic king, James VII of Scotland and II of England (died 1701), and of his son, James Francis Edward Stuart (the 'Old Pretender'). The name derived from Jacobus, Latin for 'James'.

A·NOBLE·RUIN

Bereft of residents and soldiers, Urquhart soon fell into decay. But attitudes changed, and the ancient castle came to be viewed as a noble ruin in a majestic setting.

When the last garrison marched out, the castle buildings rapidly fell into decay. People from the glen came and salvaged what they could for use elsewhere - the best of the stonework, lead from the roofs, timber, ironwork, and so forth. The death knell for the ancient stronghold was sounded on 19 February 1715, when part of the Grant Tower came crashing to the ground during a violent storm. The gaping hole in one side of the tower house bears witness to that unfortunate event.

Thereafter, time and weather wrought their slow but cumulative effect on the fabric. A survey of the castle and grounds made about 1770 shows the ancient castle buildings roofless. But it also shows a long, narrow building immediately beyond the castle ditch at the very north end of the site, close to where the large corn-kiln remains today. Presumably somebody had received the Grants' permission to 'move in'.

By then perceptions were slowly changing about the value of crumbling ruins like Urquhart. Encouraged by the writings of Sir Walter Scott and others, people began to take a greater interest in their history, and to appreciate that ruins in the landscape had a worth beyond their value as builders' salvage yards. The noble ruin beside Loch Ness, set against one of the most dramatic of Highland landscapes, drew an increasing number of visitors, to gaze in awe, to think on times past, to sketch and to paint.

Stop, Artist! with your sketching-book,
For gin ye can but tak' it,
At Urquhart Castle ye should look,
'Tis close to Drumnadrochit!

(Reverend Drake's contribution to the visitors' book
at the Drumnadrochit Inn, July 1857)

(above) Urquhart Castle and Loch Ness in the nineteenth century, by an unknown artist
(Courtesy of the Royal Commission on the Ancient and Historical Monuments of Scotland)
(left) Urquhart Castle from above Urquhart Bay (Photograph © Colin Baxter)

STATE·CARE

In time this awakening of interest in the built heritage led the Grant family to seek better ways of securing their castle's future. In 1884, Caroline, Countess Dowager of Seafield, widow of the seventh earl of Grant, assumed control of her son's estates, including Urquhart and Glenmoriston, following his untimely death. When she too died, in 1911, her will instructed that Urquhart Castle be entrusted into State care. On 6 October 1913, a guardianship agreement was signed between the late Dowager's Trustees and the Commissioners of His Majesty's Works and Public Buildings transferring responsibility for the castle's upkeep.

Her obituary in The Times noted that:

'...every function of a great landlord was splendidly performed by her, and she will be remembered with affection and respect. She was the greatest owner of woodlands in the United Kingdom, and it is computed that the number of pine trees planted by her husband, her son and herself amounted to 50,000,000 in Strathspey and Aviemore alone'.

Caroline, Countess Dowager of Seafield

'The preservation of the ruins of the said castle is a matter of public interest by reason of the historic, traditional and artistic interest attaching thereto'.

(from the 1913 Deed of Guardianship)

Historic Scotland, as successors to His Majesty's Office of Works and Public Buildings, continues to maintain the ancient ruins to this day.

URQUHART CASTLE.		£ s. d.
Approximate Estimate for Repairs, etc.		
Yds.Feet.	Gate House.	
730	Sup. Raking out and pointing joints of masonry.	) 4/- 146 0 0
55	" Cleaning tops of walls & waterproof- ing.	) 3/- 8 15 0

Extract from the repairs schedule drawn up in 1912 by His Majesty's Office of Works. The Trustees of the late Countess Dowager of Seafield contributed the princely sum of £150 towards the estimated cost of repair - £1921 19s 0d

Urquhart Castle from the north-east
(Photograph © Colin Baxter)

Storm clouds over Loch Ness
    (Mike Brooks)